W9-BBF-843

# Mercury

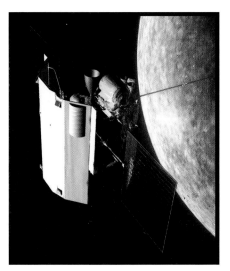

by
## Christine Taylor-Butler

Children's Press
An Imprint of Scholastic Inc.
New York  Toronto  London  Auckland  Sydney
Mexico City  New Delhi  Hong Kong
Danbury, Connecticut

These content vocabulary word builders
are for grades 1–2.

Consultant: Michelle Yehling, Astronomy Education Consultant

Photo Credits:

Photographs © 2008: Finley Holiday Film: back cover; NASA: 5 top left, 15 top, 15 bottom, 17 (Jet Propulsion Laboratory), 1, 5 bottom right, 19 (John Hopkins University Applied Physics Laboratory/Carnegie Institution of Washington); Photo Researchers, NY: 11 (Chris Butler), 4 top, 13 (Lynette Cook), 4 bottom left, 14 (Ted Kinsman), 4 bottom right (David Nunuk/SPL), cover, 2, 5 top right, 7, 23 (U.S. Geological Survey/SPL), 5 bottom left, 9 (Detlev van Ravenswaay); PhotoDisc/Getty Images via SODA: 23 left.

Illustration Credit:

Illustration pages 20–21 by Greg Harris

Book Design: Simonsays Design!
Book Production: The Design Lab

Library of Congress Cataloging-in-Publication Data
Taylor-Butler, Christine.
Mercury / by Christine Taylor-Butler.—Updated ed.
   p. cm.—(Scholastic news nonfiction readers)
Includes bibliographical references and index.
ISBN-13: 978-0-531-14698-9 (lib. bdg.)      978-0-531-14763-4 (pbk.)
ISBN-10: 0-531-14698-7 (lib. bdg.)      0-531-14763-0 (pbk.)
1. Mercury (Planet)—Juvenile literature. I. Title.
QB611.T39 2007
523.41—dc22      2006102771

1 2 3 4 5 6 7 8 9 10 R   17 16 15 14 13 12 11 10 09 08

# CONTENTS

# WORD HUNT

Look for these words as you read. They will be in **bold**.

**core**
(kor)

**meteorite**
(**mee**-tee-ur-ite)

**moon**
(moon)

**craters**
(**kray**-turz)

**Mercury**
(**muhr**-kyur-ree)

**solar system**
(**soh**-lur **siss**-tuhm)

**space probe**
(spayss prohb)

# Mercury!

Can you sing on **Mercury**?

No. You cannot sing on Mercury.

You can't even breathe. Mercury has no air.

No one has ever seen the
other side of Mercury.

Mercury is the planet closest to the Sun.

Mercury is the smallest planet in the **solar system**.

Mercury

Sun

The side of the planet that faces the Sun is boiling hot.

The side that faces away from the Sun is freezing cold.

**Mercury is only 36 million miles from the Sun.**

Mercury is made mostly of iron.

It has a very big **core** for such a little planet.

Scientists think part of the core is made of liquid iron.

core

crust

13

Mercury looks like Earth's **moon**.

Mercury and the Moon both have many **craters**.

Most of the craters were made millions of years ago.

Many of the craters were made by **meteorites**.

meteorite

crater on
Mercury

crater on
Earth's moon

One of the largest craters on Mercury is called the Caloris Basin.

It was made by an asteroid, a large rocky object, that hit Mercury.

The entire state of Texas could fit inside the Caloris Basin.

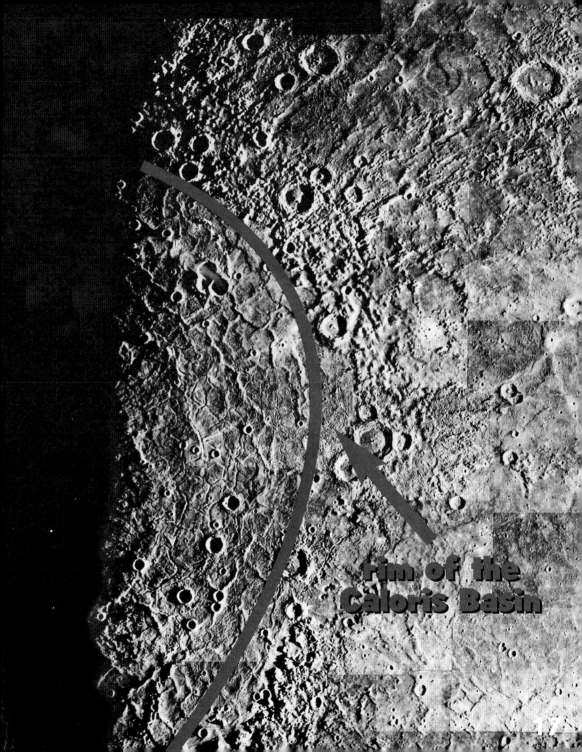

Rim of the
Caloris Basin

17

Scientists know some facts about Mercury because of a **space probe** called *Mariner 10*.

In 1975, *Mariner 10* finished its job.

Another space probe, *MESSENGER*, will arrive near Mercury in 2011.

You cannot go to Mercury. Aren't you glad that space probes can?

MESSENGER

A space probe does
not carry people.

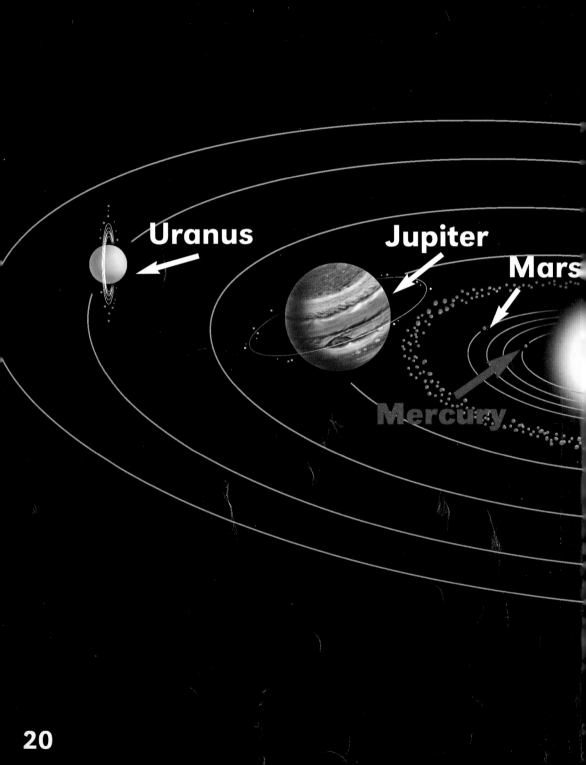

Uranus

Jupiter

Mars

Mercury

# MERCURY

## IN OUR SOLAR SYSTEM

Sun

Venus

Earth

Saturn

Neptune

# YOUR NEW WORDS

**core** (kor) the inside of an object

**craters** (**kray**-turz) large dents or holes in an object

**Mercury** (**muhr**-kyur-ree) a planet named after the Roman messenger of the gods

**meteorite** (**mee**-tee-ur-ite) a rock made of metal and stone that comes from outer space and lands on a planet or moon

**moon** (moon) an object that circles a planet

**solar system** (**soh**-lur **siss**-tuhm) the group of planets, moons, and other things that travel around the Sun

**space probe** (spayss prohb) a vehicle with robotic equipment used to explore space

# Earth and Mercury

A year is how long it takes a planet to go around the Sun.

 **1 Earth year =365 days**

 **1 Mercury year =88 Earth days**

A day is how long it takes a planet to turn one time.

 **1 Earth day = 24 hours**

 **1 Mercury day = 1,408 Earth hours**

A moon is an object that circles a planet.

 **Earth has 1 moon.**

**Mercury has no moons.**

**The Sun can rise on Mercury two times in one day.**

# INDEX

## FIND OUT MORE

**Book:**
Burnham, Robert. *Children's Atlas of the Universe*. Pleasantville, NY: Reader's Digest Children's Publishing, Inc., 2000.

**Web site:**
Solar System Exploration
*http://sse.jpl.nasa.gov/planets*

## MEET THE AUTHOR

**Christine Taylor-Butler** is the author of more than twenty books for children. She holds a degree in Engineering from M.I.T. She lives in Kansas City with her family, where they have a telescope for searching the skies.